Wade in the Water

52 Reflections on
The Faith We Sing

Martha Whitmore Hickman

ABINGDON PRESS
Nashville

Library of Congress Cataloging-in-Publication Data

Hickman, Martha Whitmore, 1925-
  Wade in the water : 52 reflections on the faith we sing / Martha Whitmore Hickman.
    p. cm.
  Includes index.
    ISBN 0-687-02797-7 (pbk.: alk. paper)
  1. United Methodist Church (U.S.)—Hymns—History and criticism.
  2. Hymns, English—History and criticism. 3. Meditations. I. Title.
  BV310 .H53 2003
  264'.076023—dc21

                                                              2002154786

Scripture quotations, unless otherwise noted, are from the New Revised Standard Version of the Bible, copyright © 1989, by the Division of Christian Education of the National Council of the Churches of Christ in the United States of America. Used by permission.

03 04 05 06 07 08 09 10 11 12—10 9 8 7 6 5 4 3 2 1
MANUFACTURED IN THE UNITED STATES OF AMERICA

For Hoyt—who else?
Husband,
Advisor,
who helped put together The Faith We Sing—
with love and appreciation

Contents

Preface

When given the opportunity to write reflections on fifty-two of the two hundred and eighty-four hymns, songs, and choruses in *The Faith We Sing,* how does one go about choosing? And why fifty-two? The latter is a simpler question to answer: Because there are fifty-two Sundays in the year, and because choir directors are among the people for whom this book is intended—to use, perhaps, in a devotional moment as choir practice gets underway. Or if one of these hymns, songs, or choruses is to be introduced to the congregation on a coming Sunday, the reading of the accompanying reflection may be part of the choir's preparation as they practice that particular song. Apart from its relevance to the fifty-two Sundays of the year, individuals who treasure particular songs may want to use this book, with its scripture readings, reflections, and prayers, in their personal devotions.

Again, why, given free reign, did I choose *these* fifty-two? I wanted some balance, of course, in the cultures that are represented here: African American spirituals, as in "Wade in the Water"; a West Indian carol, as in "The Virgin Mary Had a Baby Boy"; a song where the words are printed both in English and in another language, as in "Song of Hope *(Canto de Esperanza),*" in addition to many songs of European American origin.

I chose songs with a variety of images for God, as in "Bring Many Names"; songs that ask penetrating questions, as in "Here Am I"; songs with a compelling rhythm, as in "Woke Up This Morning"; and then a song that seems to encapsulate the whole Christian life story: "I Was There to Hear Your Borning Cry." How could I leave *that* out?

Some I chose because personal associations have led me to love them: "A Mother Lined a Basket" takes me back to childhood, when my parents gave me a small porcelain baby doll in a lined wicker basket. Being a child of Sunday school and Bible stories, I named the doll Moses, and I treasured this gift for many years. "The Lily of the Valley" calls to mind the bed of lilies of the valley (my mother's favorite flower) that grew year after year on the north side of our home, and which, in their season, I passed each day going to and from school.

And some I have chosen because their imagery is so gripping that, being the word person that I am, I could not pass them up: "She Comes Sailing on the Wind"; "God the Sculptor of the Mountains"; "His Eye Is on the Sparrow," which, in addition to its compelling image, brings with it the echo of Ethel Waters' voice singing the song.

Are these reasons for choosing too idiosyncratic, too personal? For some, they may be. But music, as we know from the way songs often drift, unbidden, into our minds, speaks to us at a deeply emotional level, speaks to our personal and corporate history, to our memories, to our anxieties and our hopes, and it is in response to some often indefinable summons that a song may call us to itself.

So may you find, in these fifty-two reflections, old friends freshly appreciated and new friends illumined; and as we sing these songs, may we come home to our faith and to our life, so that as we walk among others, "They'll Know We Are Christians by Our Love."

We Sing to You, O God

#2001 in *The Faith We Sing*

Make a joyful noise to God, all the earth; / sing the glory of his name . . . / Say to God, "How awesome are your deeds! . . . / All the earth worships you; / they sing praises to you, / sing praises to your name."

Psalm 66:1-4

This is a song of praise to God, sung from full hearts for all that God has given. It begins with a series of images of caregiving, starting with "the Rock who gave us birth."

Then the Israelites confess that they wandered far from home, out into the desert, but God protected them from the storms and kept them safe, shielding them from fear, carrying them in the sheltering arms of love.

Like a mother eagle, God lifts them and bears them toward the sun, carrying them along to the light and air they need, but also, as they need it, covering them with the protection of God's wings. These are wonderful images of God's creation, caregiving, and tender love, of God's protection from the storm and from falling before we are ready to fly on our own.

Singers of this hymn may be reminded of other hymns and songs celebrating God's creation, and God's love and care—as a mother eagle cares for her young, as a protector and rescuer when God's people inadvertently wander into the desert before they know how to cope with its rigors. Yet God is always there, ready to protect and save.

So of course the Israelites sing their gratitude and praise! And so do we.

Prayer: O God, who dost hold all creation in the hollow of your hand, we lift to you our songs of praise and thanksgiving. Amen.

Praise the Source of Faith and Learning

#2004 in *The Faith We Sing*

Then Jesus said . . . "And you will know the truth, and the truth will make you free."

John 8:31-32

This hymn presents in varied images a conflict that raises its head in various guises at different times in our lives, the conflict we sometimes feel between faith and knowledge—or as it is sometimes put, between religion and science.

On whichever side of this river of speculation we find ourselves, there are always questions for which we have no answers. I recall my young son, perhaps three years old, saying softly to himself, "I wonder, wonder, wonder who made God." Questions begin early, and they last a long time.

What this hymn expresses so well is that we live by faith, but it is a faith always in search of more knowledge, more discernment. There is no way we are going to fully understand the meshings of science, art, knowledge, and faith. But we *can* ask God to keep us from making harmful blunders in insisting on truths of which we have no ultimate knowledge, and at the same time to keep us ever alert to wonders that at any moment may manifest God's hand at work, God's Spirit infusing our spirit.

It is a high wire balancing act, this blending of faith and learning, and we may fall to one side or the other many times. But, if we are willing, God will return us to our searchings and will steady our feet along the way, so that faith and learning may enrich one another, until, like a flowing river, "they join as one, returning praise and thanks to you, their Source."

Prayer: O thou Source of all knowledge and all faith, make us brave in asking questions and open to the empowerment of our faith in you and your faith in us. Amen.

Let All Things Now Living

#2008 in *The Faith We Sing*

"The LORD went in front of them in a pillar of cloud by day, to lead them along the way, and in a pillar of fire by night, to give them light, so that they might travel by day and by night. Neither the pillar of cloud by day nor the pillar of fire by night left its place in front of the people."
Exodus 13:21-22

Many of us are familiar with this melody from singing it with a different set of words at camps and youth gatherings, as "The Ash Grove"—and the differentness here may be a little disconcerting at first. But as we sing these words, perhaps those early experiences of fellowship and of celebrating nature in song will add another layer of joyous thanksgiving to this hymn, which celebrates the trustworthiness and inventiveness and constancy of God.

Think of what it must have been like for the Hebrews, wandering in the desert, longing for a home, to see at the front of their column of march such signs that were unmistakably from God, for how could it be otherwise that day after day, night after night, the cloud by day and the pillar of fire by night moved before them, leading them on?

These signs of God's leading, direct and unmistakable, extend the trust and recognition of the wanderers, and of subsequent generations, to the orderliness of God's creation as observed in other natural phenomena—to the reliability of "stars in their courses and sun in its orbit . . . the deeps of the ocean [that] proclaim the Divine." All of these signs of order are signs of God's trustworthiness. So may we, too, unite with all the rest of creation in singing glad hymns to the God who created us and protects us, and who shows us, even now, the path we should follow, in love and in praise!

Prayer: God of the cloud, God of the fire, we lift our songs of gratitude and praise. Amen.

Let Us with a Joyful Mind

#2012 in *The Faith We Sing*

O give thanks to the God of heaven, / for his steadfast love endures forever.

Psalm 136:26

You may recognize this hymn as an adaptation of John Milton's poem, which begins with "Let us, with a gladsome mind." The poem itself is based on Psalm 136.

The words also call to mind the creation story found in the first chapter of Genesis: the creation of the sun, moon, and stars, the creatures of the sea and the land—a recapitulation of the earlier stages of creation. In the hymn, there is no specific mention of man or woman apart from the rest of creation.

In Psalm 136, the refrain that follows each enumeration of God's goodness is "for his steadfast love endures forever." In "Let Us with a Joyful Mind," the refrain is adapted only slightly to highlight the fullness of God's mercy and faithfulness toward us.

This is but one example of how the arts inform and enrich one another. We think of the stories of David in the Bible, and we see in our mind's eye Michelangelo's gleaming sculpture. And think of all the Christmas pageants you have seen in which the story of Christ's birth is acted out, from Mary and Joseph arriving at one inn after another only to be turned away, to the softly illuminated scene of the baby (a real baby? a doll?) on a bed of straw, the doting parents gazing down in love.

So do we with "joyful mind" find ways to celebrate and honor creation and the God who made us.

Prayer: Creator of all that is, we rejoice in your being, and the life you have given us. Amen.

Womb of Life

#2046 in *The Faith We Sing*

And the Word became flesh and lived among us, and we have seen his glory, the glory as of a father's only son, full of grace and truth.

John 1:14

This wonderful hymn, with its initial startling image, conveys an ultimate sense of security and hope—as a mother and father wait in hope for the birth of a child, snugly cradled in the mother's womb.

Then the imagery shifts in the second verse to describe Jesus as our brother, born to bring new birth to us—Jesus who stands among us, shares our life with all its beauty and fragility—and then to the "Risen Christ," who, breathing his Spirit upon us, gives us new life, new hope.

The plea is to this Risen Christ, this "Brooding Spirit," who will work with us, upholding us in our weakness, reminding us who and whose we are and, in turn, helping us give birth to the new world of love and freedom he personifies.

And then in stanza four, the hymn addresses the triune God, in the many roles in which God comes to us. At different times in our lives, and under different circumstances, we need God in one—or several—of these roles. The hymn tells us that Jesus stands ready to receive us, to work with us, to fulfill our every need; and we, in turn, yearn to join him, singing, praising, reveling in a world made new in him, our risen and ever-present Lord.

Prayer: For our ultimate confidence in you, we give you thanks. For your boundless hope that we will turn to you, we give you thanks. For your arms outstretched in welcome, and for our halting, hopeful, and strengthening steps toward you, we give you thanks. Amen.

13

Bring Many Names

#2047 in *The Faith We Sing*

For a child has been born for us, / a son given to us / . . . and he is named / Wonderful Counselor, Mighty God, / Everlasting Father, Prince of Peace.

Isaiah 9:6

I am reminded, as I read the words of this hymn, of some words a layperson in our church spoke in preaching a sermon (perhaps on Laity Sunday): "If you need a father, God will be your father. If you need a mother, God will be your mother. If you need a child, God will be your child." I found his words moving then, as I do now—and have, over the years.

Some of the words of this hymn, as did those words of the lay preacher, describe a God different from the one we are accustomed to. And yet what fresh insights they bring to us—that God is not only the "Wonderful Counselor, Mighty God, Everlasting Father, Prince of Peace," but that God is present in each one of us, and, in God's being, all our attributes are included.

There is something wonderfully endearing in these portraits of God, moving away from the stereotypes that often fill our thoughts of God. Some people find that the image of "strong mother God" is perhaps not so startling in this day as we are gratefully acknowledging that God can nurture us as well as be strong for us. Equally loving is the image of "warm father God," whom many of us have known in our experience of our earthly father.

But the real stunner, it seems to me, is in the fourth stanza, wherein we hear of a God advanced in age, who both feels and outwardly shows the weight of concern and care for our well-being. What a welcome stretch this gives to the imagination—that wherever we are in our own life cycle, in whatever state of age or health we are, God inhabits that terrain with us and keeps us on the alert for "good

14

surprises." May it be so for us, that we feel God's presence at such moments, as at all moments.

Prayer: All-embracing God, we sing with all your people, "Hail and Hosannah, great, living God!" Amen.

Mothering God,
You Gave Me Birth

#2050 in *The Faith We Sing*

"Jerusalem, Jerusalem. . . . How often have I desired to gather your children together as a hen gathers her brood under her wings."

Luke 13:34

One could hardly find an image of God more supportive of the mothering aspects of God than in the writings of Juliana of Norwich, reflected in this hymn. Some people feel that this idea of God as having qualities of a mother is a modern invention and somehow dangerous, not to be trusted. But think, Juliana of Norwich lived in the fifteenth century; she is the first non-anonymous woman whose writings in English have survived. Hardly a modern notion, then, that our God can be likened to a mother in addition to a father. In Luke 13:34, the image Jesus used was that of a mother hen, eagerly holding her young close, keeping them warm against her own body.

In this hymn we see the three persons of the Trinity: God the Creator, in motherly form; Christ, represented in the Communion—the "bread and the cup," the ultimate gift of Christ's body; and the Holy Spirit, holding us close as we struggle with our own uncertain faith.

One of the endearing qualities of the writings of Juliana is her admission of her own faltering in the faith: One minute she is sure of the truth of the gospel; the next minute she is thrown into tortuous doubt; and then, with great relief, she recovers her faith in full. Can you imagine a better figure than a mother to hold and comfort you, to be a steadying, assuring presence while you go through your journey—as you find yourself alternately triumphant, then fearfully uncertain, then rejoicing and confident once more?

Prayer: God who has given us birth, may we celebrate your being in all its manifestations. Amen.

I Was There to Hear Your Borning Cry

#2051 in *The Faith We Sing*

For it was you who formed my inward parts; / you knit me together in my mother's womb. . . . / In your book were written / all the days that were formed for me . . . / I come to the end—I am still with you.

Psalm 139:13, 16, 18

This has been referred to as a "four-hankie hymn," perhaps because it poignantly describes our fondest wishes—that at each step in our life, from birth to death, God is present, meeting us in the event or stage of life in a way in which we would most covet God's presence.

The hymn is quite remarkable in the way it follows our life cycle in a manner that identifies the passages and at the same time allows for individual choices and personal responses. Any of us who have given birth can remember the thrill of that heart-stopping first cry. Any parent of an adolescent—or a young person caught in adolescent anguish—will recognize the emotional and physical upheaval of a young man or woman struggling for independence.

Then it moves through the uncertainties of choosing a mate and the adjustments and joys of becoming responsible and joyous life partners.

The quandaries of middle life are here; when we wonder what our life will become. In stanza five, the reassurance that God will guide us through the night, surely reduces the scariness of what may lie ahead.

And then in the sixth stanza, there is the coming of death and the unknown, with God's promise to be there, as always, with a final surprise. What more could we ask for than God's benevolent presence being with us in that moment of the unknowable?

If this is indeed "a four-hankie hymn," the tears must be tears of joy.

Prayer: Eternal God, you who stand with us in the myriad adventures of our lives, be with us now, to share in our gratitude for this hymn of confidence and praise. Amen.

The Lone, Wild Bird

#2052 in *The Faith We Sing*

How weighty to me are your thoughts, O God! / How vast is the sum of them! / I try to count them—they are more than the sand; / I come to the end—I am still with you.

Psalm 139:17-18

Here the psalmist is describing a God to whom all things are known, whose knowledge encompasses creation—no matter how remote and solitary its manifestations: even a lone wild bird is fully known to God. In the hymn, too, we have a God to whom all is known, from the depths of the sea and the farthest reaches of the earth, to the earliest moments of the creation of each human being, a God who lovingly made each of us and knew us by name before we were born. How comforting it is, to each of us as to the hymn writer, to think of God knowing us this intimately.

Being known this intimately brings responsibility, too. As the hymn writer rests in the knowledge that God is constantly with him—has known him since before he was conceived—he also recognizes that God knows of his imperfections. And he prays that God will show him these shortcomings, will bring into his life new life and the healing of his spirit. So may it be for us.

But underlying his knowledge that he is far from perfect is the more important knowledge that whatever happens to him, whatever shortcomings he has, the God who knew him before he was born, who knows him to the depths of his being will be with him always—constant, loving, welcoming, present with him through all his life. And in his death? Resting with him in that great unknown venture, too, speaking his name, as present to him as breath.

Prayer: Great Spirit, we are yours. Come, rest in us, too. Amen.

I Am Your Mother

#2059 in *The Faith We Sing*

Then the LORD God formed man from the dust of the ground, and breathed into his nostrils the breath of life; and the man became a living being.

Genesis 2:7

We come from the earth. We are formed from the dust of the earth. We have a common destiny with the earth. If the earth perishes, if we do not take care of it, so shall human beings perish. In some ways the thought of our being so interdependent seems remote much of the time.

But then, as my husband and I did with Hurricane Mitch, we see the ravages that flood the towns, homes, and gardens; or we see how the churchyard at the end of our street is flooded after a heavy rain, and we are brought up sharp to the fact that the earth's destiny is our destiny.

Some so-called natural disasters are, at least so far, beyond our control. We cannot control the turmoil that comes out of the sky, though we have made marvelous strides in weather prediction, so that areas in danger can be evacuated and life preserved. We cannot control the fierce rumblings of the deep earth that create earthquakes, leaving death and destruction in their wake, though we are constantly studying the mechanics of rocks deep below the surface of the earth, and we have building codes that, when followed, greatly minimize the loss of life.

But there is much we can do to preserve and protect the earth, our home and the source of our being; and though it is often half-heartedly, we are learning to conserve our fuel, to refrain from feeding the earth with poisonous chemicals, to reforest our scarred hillsides. But we do not do enough: "I am your mother, tears on my face."

Prayer: God, help us to care for the earth with loving hearts and respect so that she will be preserved. Amen.

God the Sculptor
of the Mountains

#2060 in *The Faith We Sing*

In the beginning when God created the heavens and the earth, the earth was a formless void and darkness covered the face of the deep, while a wind from God swept over the face of the waters.

Genesis 1:1-2

This hymn represents God in many roles—many, but not all, having to do with creation. And then, in the last line of each stanza, there is a plea to God for help in our shortcomings, and in our needs.

I am writing this reflection in an isolated cabin on a mountainside in north Georgia. The dogwood is beginning to bloom. Trails lead up and down the mountain, the ground is covered with a mix of loose gravel and fallen leaves. I am far from the city, and as darkness fall here the stars glisten across the night sky. It is easy to revere God the Creator—"womb of all creation," as the hymn writer puts it.

But then I am startled to read the first line of the second stanza: "God the nuisance to the Pharaoh," and, farther down, "God the beacon of the free." So I am reminded, in this idyllic setting, not only of God the creator of mountains and seas, grain and vineyard, but also of the social aspects of God's will for us, and of our history of deserved unrest—"God the table-turning prophet."

So this hymn gathers, in wonderful inclusiveness, the many aspects of God and of our life together. We see God the creator of this most beautiful world, and here and there, lest we forget the troubling parts of our history, are reminders to be aware of the need for justice, too. The best way to do that? "You are present every moment, we are searching; meet us now."

Prayer: God, the sculptor of all this beautiful world, we praise you for the wonders of your creation. Keep us aware of the needs of others, too. Amen.

The Lily of the Valley

#2062 in *The Faith We Sing*

"I do not call you servants any longer, because the servant does not know what the master is doing; but I have called you friends, because I have made known to you everything that I have heard from my Father."

John 15:15

Think of your closest friend—a person whose presence you long for when you are feeling down or confused or lonely, when you don't necessarily need advice, you just need "somebody to talk to."

And you tell your friend what's on your mind, and your heart is lightened, and you feel ready to go on. The objective situation may not change at all, but how much better you feel, having shared your feelings, no matter how "unimportant" they may be. And how much more able you are to deal with whatever issues come up—arguments you can just as well avoid, times when you might otherwise make a wrong choice or let some past mistake weigh like lead on your mind.

Then think of this friendship as multiplied ten-thousandfold: nothing need be held back, because the friend will understand what is going on with you at the deepest level and will love you still. And furthermore, the presence of this friend will be available to you forever, closer than breathing, nearer than hands and feet. It is this kind of friendship with Jesus that this hymn writer points us toward when we sing, "He's the Lily of the Valley, the bright and Morning Star."

Each of us brings our own history to the hymns we sing. When I sing this song I think of a bed of lilies of the valley that lay along the north side of our house. They were my mother's favorite flower, and often, on my way home from elementary school, I stooped to inhale their fragrance as I passed them on my way to the love and security of home.

Prayer: Eternal God, help us to accept the gifts overflowing that you offer us in friendship with Jesus, "the Lily of the Valley, the bright and Morning Star." Amen.

O Lord, You're Beautiful

#2064 in *The Faith We Sing*

Hear, O LORD, when I cry aloud, / be gracious to me and answer me! / "Come," my heart says, "seek his face!" / Your face, LORD, do I seek. / Do not hide your face from me.
Psalm 27:7-9

This is, at first glance, a very simple hymn, but it has great power.

Think back over your life to the most precious, most loving faces you have known. Are there people in your memory who, just to look upon their faces, bring blessings you had not expected but will probably never forget? If these are people you have known and loved, to look on their faces is to experience a richness and gratitude that touches you deeply.

I recall waiting to meet my husband at some previously designated place. I got there first, and he didn't see me right away. But I saw him coming and felt my heart swell with love and anticipation of simply being with him again. Often that memory comes to mind when I read or sing the words of this hymn. I feel I know a fraction of what it would be to behold the face of Jesus, and as the words of the hymn suggest, I know that his eyes are upon me and that I am filled with his grace.

It is the same with touch—the healing of fatigue, of tension, of pain. We know how the loving touch of a mother or father can calm and heal a child. If we experience this healing from human beings we love, what would the healing touch of Jesus be?

Prayer: O Lord, you're beautiful. May your grace abound in me, so that I may pass on some of your healing beauty to others. Amen.

O Blessed Spring

#2076 in *The Faith We Sing*

"I am the vine, you are the branches. Those who abide in me and I in them bear much fruit, because apart from me you can do nothing."

John 15:5

This hymn uses the familiar image of Christ as the central Vine and Christians as the branches. With that basic figure the hymn describes the various stages of our own life against the greening and eventual withering of the vine—but with the important difference that while the vine may end its season in death, we, as we approach the withering season, will find fresh nourishment in the Word and the water promised by Christ, and thus enter God's Tree of Life anew.

The season of the vine begins in the spring, the time when symbolically, Christians attach themselves to Christ, the Tree of Life. The next phase of our human cycle, parallel to summer heat, takes us through the rebellion and uncertainty of youth, sustained nonetheless by "rain" from Christ, which, in both the tumultuous youth and the drooping vine, brings new life.

When autumn comes and youth is past, the harvest is rich and the soul seems to have attained some welcome equilibrium. And then winter comes, and though the vines may wither, even as we draw our last breath, "our souls take wing and trust the promise of the spring."

Finally, the figure of Christ as the Vine is praised for this mystery by which what appeared to be dead is joined again to the Tree of Life. Christ, the true Vine, and we, the branches, are given additional meaning—in the seasons of gardening, and of life.

Prayer: Gardener, Life-giver, the One True Vine, we give, day by day, our life into your hands. Amen.

Woke Up This Morning

#2082 in *The Faith We Sing*

I wait for the Lord, *my soul waits, / and in his word I hope; / my soul waits for the* Lord / *more than those who watch for the morning, / more than those who watch for the morning.*

Psalm 130:5-6

We all know what a difference our waking mood casts over the early part of any day. If we have had a bad dream, it takes a while to get over the effect that dream still extends into our life. If it has been a particularly good dream, it may take a while to come down from that elation and face reality!

But here is one hymn writer who, on waking, was thinking of Jesus, and who continues to sing hallelujahs in the aftermath of that dream. The hymn goes on, in succeeding stanzas, to extol the virtues of keeping your mind "stayed on Jesus"—whether or not Jesus was in your thoughts on first waking.

If you hate your neighbor, such feelings cannot last if you replace them with thoughts of Jesus.

Your capacity to love everybody will swell to the edges of your brain if you fill it with thoughts of Jesus.

If you keep your thoughts "stayed on Jesus," the devil is not going to catch you off guard, because there will be no room for evil and destructive thoughts.

And finally, to ensure your safety from wrongdoing—well, if Jesus is the captain of your mind, he will see to it that you do no wrong. But you will have to obey him!

Prayer: God, keep us single-minded in bringing all of our day's activities and thoughts before your loving judgment. Amen.

The Snow Lay on the Ground

#2093 in *The Faith We Sing*

While they were there, the time came for her to deliver her child. And she gave birth to her firstborn son and wrapped him in bands of cloth, and laid him in a manger.

Luke 2:6-7

What is startling about this hymn, if we are attentive to the words of the first phrase, is how far from reality the words are: "The snow lay on the ground"? Snow? In Bethlehem? What about all those pictures of shepherds on a hillside with their grazing flocks; of Mary and Joseph arriving at the inn, and, finally, at the stable, in clothing which surely has no suggestion of snowy weather; of the infant Christ wrapped in "bands of cloth"? No hint of snow in any of these.

Yet we who live in northern climes, as likely did the writer of this "Anglo-English carol," often observe the Christmas season with snow all around us. How brightly the Christmas lights cast their color over the white gleam of snow! "I hope we have snow for Christmas!" we say to one another. "I'm dreaming of a white Christmas," goes the familiar song.

Is there some kind of important discrepancy here? Of course not. Christ is for all seasons, all cultures, all climates. It is the event, not the weather, that we're celebrating. Perhaps the very unlikelihood that the hymn's words are tied to actual fact underscores the universality of its message: "Venite adoremus Dominum"—"O come, let us adore him, Christ the Lord." The "inaccuracy" of the weather described is no more inappropriate than using Latin rather than Aramaic, the common language of Jesus' time, to lift our praise to God.

And if we long to have angels in "the heavenly host" connected to a scene of snow lying on the ground, well—we can join the children in lying down and making "angels" in the snow!

Prayer: God of all nations, of all times and places, accept our gratitude, offered in Jesus' name. Amen.

The Virgin Mary Had a Baby Boy

#2098 in *The Faith We Sing*

And she gave birth to her firstborn son and wrapped him in bands of cloth, and laid him in a manger.

Luke 2:7

The scripture quoted above (which also appears with the previous reflection) is only a small portion of the story this West Indian carol celebrates with such buoyancy and joy. To recall the whole story would take up virtually the entire page, so you are urged to read once again the whole of Luke's account as background to appreciating this carol. (See Luke 2:1-20.)

The story is told in calypso rhythm. The verses, while in no way staid, are fairly straightforward in telling the basic fact of the baby's birth and the speculation that his name is Jesus.

But then! Excitement and rapture take over in the refrain, repeated after each chapter of the familiar story. First comes the singing of the angels, celebrating the holy birth, followed by the rapturous refrain. Then a stanza tells of the arrival of the shepherds—no details are given, and none are necessary; the refrain again tells all that's needed and we know the place of glory from which this holy infant has come.

Then the Wise Men came, adding to the miraculous story, and the repeated announcement that the baby's name is Jesus. And, once again, the jubilant refrain. No calm, sedate, reverential tones here, though there is reverence enough in the message of the carol. But this music, these exclamations of glory—they are enough to set our feet to dancing.

And they often do!

Prayer: Eternal God, in whose domain are laughter and exuberance and dancing, we celebrate the birth of Jesus with our brothers and sisters around the world. Amen.

Joseph Dearest, Joseph Mine

#2099 in *The Faith We Sing*

Joseph also went . . . to the city of David called Bethlehem. . . . He went to be registered with Mary, to whom he was engaged and who was expecting a child. While they were there, the time came for her to deliver her child. And she gave birth to her firstborn son and wrapped him in bands of cloth, and laid him in a manger.

Luke 2:4-7

This has been a favorite Christmas hymn, not only for the lovely melody and words, but probably because it includes Joseph as a beloved character in the Christmas story, which so commonly focuses on Mary.

Here the first stanza is as sung by Mary, asking the child's father—as would any new mother—for help in caring for this new baby, but addressing him with such tenderness that one knows of her love for him.

And then we have Joseph in the second stanza, gladly acceding to his beloved's request to "help with the baby." He too recognizes the special quality of this child, as well as his own inclusion in the story: "God's own light on us both shall shine in paradise, as prays the mother Mary." Yes, her role in the birth of the child is more important than his, but he is part of the story too, and one can imagine them joining in the refrain—and again in the third stanza—in love and tenderness, acknowledging the role of this special child, to whose infant care they both are happily devoted.

This is an altogether lovable carol, and it adds a note of Joseph's participation that is often overlooked.

Prayer: Gracious God, we share with gratitude in the tenderness of this family scene. Amen.

Thou Didst Leave Thy Throne

#2100 in *The Faith We Sing*

Let the same mind be in you that was in Christ Jesus, who . . . / did not regard equality with God / as something to be exploited. . . . / And being found in human form, / he humbled himself / and became obedient to the point of death—/ even death on a cross.

Philippians 2:5-8

This hymn runs the full circle of the gospel experience. The first two stanzas tell of Christ's leaving the splendor to which his closeness to God entitled him, to enter human life as a baby born under the humblest of circumstances, in the shelter of a stable.

And then the refrain urgently offers him hospitality in the singer's heart.

In the third stanza, Jesus, now a man, wanders the Galilean roadways and hillsides, without, unlike even the lowly creatures of the forests and the air, a place to call home.

In the fourth stanza, Jesus' mission to bring freedom to the people is subverted by betrayal and crucifixion at the hands of his enemies. And again the refrain of the believer—a comfort, an invitation: Come, "there is room in my heart."

But then, in the fifth stanza, the whole of heaven rings in rejoicing at Jesus' triumphant victory over death. Now, the yearning of the believer is to be called to be with Jesus, to hear Jesus' beckoning words of assurance, "There is room at my side for thee!" And so the refrain as Jesus reaches out in welcome: "And my heart shall rejoice, Lord Jesus, when thou comest and callest for me."

It is a risk to invite Jesus into your heart, because who knows what might happen? We think of the famous—Saint Francis, Mother Teresa—whose lives are evidence of their welcoming of Jesus to take up habitation in their hearts. And of the nonfamous—a woman in New York who opens her home to babies with AIDS, people who work with those who are homeless and hungry, countless men and women and boys and girls who perform selfless acts of kindness and generosity—and we imagine Jesus calling to them, "Come to me, there is room in my heart for thee."

Prayer: God, may I live my life in gratitude for what you have given, and in expectation of gifts yet to come. Amen.

Wade in the Water

#2107 in *The Faith We Sing*

Now in Jerusalem by the Sheep Gate there is a pool. . . .
One man was there who had been ill for thirty-eight years.
When Jesus saw him lying there . . . he said to him, "Do
you want to be made well?" The sick man answered him,
"Sir, I have no one to put me into the pool when the water
is stirred up. . . . " Jesus said to him, "Stand up, take your
mat and walk." At once the man was made well, and he
took up his mat and began to walk.

John 5:2-9

What a flood of images come to mind with this hymn!
Perhaps we think of children, timidly putting a foot into a
running stream, testing whether it is safe to venture in.
Perhaps we remember times when we ourselves were testing the waters, checking on the turbulence. But in the
story, who are those hosts dressed in white and red? And
what is this about "troubling the water"?

There was a belief at the time this text was written that
angel spirits stirred up the water, and that was what made
people well—like our whirlpool baths, our natural warm
springs. But picture this person in John 5 who was ill (for
thirty-eight years!), who kept hoping he'd have his turn
and that someone would come along and help him. And
then came Jesus, who, in the immediacy of his presence,
encouraged the man to take up his mat and walk. And the
man did, and was made well.

The metaphor in the hymn tells us that God will give us
what we need, as in the stirring of the waters when God gave
Moses and the Israelites and the hosts of followers what they
needed. And sometimes, even if we've waited a long time, we
can claim the help Jesus offers, and take up our mats and walk.

Prayer: Holy God, the waters are stirring. Give us the
courage and faith to wade in, knowing you are with us.
Amen.

At the Font We Start Our Journey

#2114 in *The Faith We Sing*

Do you not know that all of us who have been baptized into Christ Jesus were baptized into his death? Therefore we have been buried with him by baptism into death, so that, just as Christ was raised from the dead by the glory of the Father, so we too might walk in newness of life.

Romans 6:3-4

This hymn could be described as a play in four acts.

The first is the act of baptism, where we are welcomed into the family of believers, joined with others who give homage to "the Easter faith." In the case of infant baptism, what the children know or feel through this experience is that someone other than their parents is holding them close; that words are being said; that a gentle hand, wet with moisture, cradles their head; and that they are loved and welcomed by a lot of people. Later, the children will learn more of what baptism means, but this act of being lovingly held, and hearing gently spoken words, and feeling the touch of water on the head, convey love in a form that is new. Not a bad start for understanding what's happening!

The second act is the service of worship, where, as the children mature—and as we mature!—the Easter story is expressed, evoked, extending our experience of the life of faith.

Act three is the service of Communion, when, by symbolic fragments of bread and juice, we share in the family meal of Holy Communion, a sign of our participation in Christ's being, our tie with the rest of the worldwide family of believers.

And in the fourth act we are sent forth to carry our mission into the world in the name and in the Spirit of Christ Jesus. Whatever our work—homemaker, writer, teacher, doctor—all have a different tone and outcome because our work, our journey, begins and goes forward in the Lord.

Prayer: God, go with us as we carry your Word into the life we live, week by week. Amen.

Spirit, Spirit of Gentleness

#2120 in *The Faith We Sing*

O Lord my God, you are very great. . . . / you ride on the
wings of the wind, / you make the winds your messengers.
Psalm 104:1-4

It is hard to imagine a hymn or song in which the many
moods of the wind are portrayed more vividly, more beau-
tifully, than they are in these lines. We have God as the one
who creates, calling the seas into the rise and fall of waters,
the rhythmic motion of tides, causing us to feel the invig-
orating sting of sand blowing on our bodies, and, around
us, calling the mountains into being "from the valleys of
sleep."

We have God as divine agitator, calling forth prophets to
open our eyes to injustice when we have become too comfortable in the lulling waft of the wind.

We have God sending forth breath as a parent singing to
a newborn in a stable; God helping us to learn from the
sorrows we have inflicted on others and endured ourselves;
God giving us new visions, new dreams, new courage to
carry out our dreams.

The poet sings of a God of swift and stinging demand for
justice, and in another mood, of a God who, in the silence,
whispers quietly in our ear, summoning us not with harsh
threats, but with a loving, gentle care. And all of this with
a gentleness that keeps us from being defensive, that
assures us God has our best interests at heart, even as we
are called to be our best selves, attending in gratitude to the
messages borne on the wind.

Prayer: Eternal, all-loving One, let us not be lulled to
apathy by your gentleness, but may our spirits be cleansed
and ready to hear what, in your many voices, you are calling us to be and to do. Amen.

She Comes Sailing on the Wind

#2122 in *The Faith We Sing*

The earth was a formless void and darkness covered the face of the deep, while a wind from God swept over the face of the waters.

Genesis 1:2

The image of the Holy Spirit as feminine may seem strange to many of us. But why?

Nowhere in the Bible are we told that the Holy Spirit is masculine, and the biblical references here to the Holy Spirit seem at least as fitting to a feminine presence—luminous, airy, likened to a gentle breeze—as to a masculine one.

And who better than another woman to help Mary through some of the uncertain moments that must have accompanied her pregnancy, telling her it was going to be all right—that the child she carried was the fulfillment of a promise of never ending peace, the reassurance of which put a song in Mary's heart.

At the occasion of Jesus' baptism, the Spirit hovered above him like a mother. We know of the voice from above, "This is my beloved Son, with whom I am well pleased." But as Jesus came up out of the water, irrevocably cast now in a new role, the comfort of a feminine Spirit would have given him added confidence and blessing. And after the darkness of the Crucifixion, the Spirit returned with the dawn, as the hymn says, with her wings opened out in flight, bringing life on a wind from God.

Prayer: Eternal God, open our hearts and our imaginations to receive your Spirit in ever-renewing form. Amen.

All Who Hunger

#2126 in *The Faith We Sing*

In the evening quails came up and covered the camp; and in the morning there was a layer of dew around the camp. When the layer of dew lifted, there on the surface of the wilderness was a fine flaky substance, as fine as frost on the ground. When the Israelites saw it, they said to one another, "What is it?" For they did not know what it was. Moses said to them, "It is the bread that the Lord has given you to eat."

Exodus 16:13-15

This story is sometimes used around Holy Communion, though it has nothing to do with the Last Supper. But it does affirm a common meal for the community, and a meal sent to them by God—manna, a meal with a meaning they do not understand. We are told in Exodus that "it was like coriander seed, white, and the taste of it was like wafers made with honey" (16:31). We know that it was to be gathered for each day's use, except on the day preceding the sabbath, when there would be enough to be gathered for two days.

The hymn extends the significance of the story—that all, even strangers, shall be welcome to this feast. And furthermore, their spirits also will be fed. They come from a state of restlessness and longing, and share in the joy of the feast. They come from a lost and scattered company, and taste, in this feast, the eternal grace of God. Thus empowered, they go forth to live lives of gratitude, to continue to share the feast of love and service, to join in songs of praise to Jesus Christ, the Living Bread.

So the story, begun with the quail and the land covered with manna, leads into the story of Christ, the Living Bread of life, offered to all who are hungry, lonely, restless, in the continuing gift of Communion: "Taste and see that God is good."

Prayer: For your gift to the Israelites, for your continuing gift to us, we give you thanks, dear Lord. Amen.

Come and Find the Quiet Center

#2128 in *The Faith We Sing*

In returning and rest you shall be saved; / in quietness and in trust shall be your strength.

Isaiah 30:15

How we all long for it: A place, a state of mind and heart, where we can feel true peace, resting with true security in a sense of God-with-us. Perhaps we have memories we return to, as holy reserves, to remind us that such elation in the Spirit really is possible, as Peter and James and John must have returned again and again in their minds to that scene of the Transfiguration, where Jesus stood before them with Elijah and Moses—sacred memories to draw on in tough times.

We yearn to have such holy moments again. But how can we bring them about? It's not that easy, when any "free time" we have has at least ten things calling to us: "Here, what about me?"

Sometimes these moments of "resting in God" come unbidden. Such moments are gifts to be cherished. More often, we have to set the stage, make the space available and clear. This hymn is full of images, "stage directions," to call us to that holy, God-embracing place within. If you have a chance, before you sing, read the words slowly to yourself, letting your imagination take you to the places the hymn suggests. And listen. Can you hear God speak your name? Can you feel the absolute empathy of One who knows what is in your heart and mind?

Then sing the song, and what a surprise! In all the confusion and turmoil of your life, you may find yourself in that place of deep reflection where, no matter how busy and preoccupied you are, the Spirit will see to it that there is always more than enough room. Perhaps right now, you will know in some timeless way that you are in the presence of God.

Prayer: I am listening, God. I am breathing deeply. And deep within me I think I hear you calling my name.

When Cain Killed Abel

#2135 in *The Faith We Sing*

Cain said to his brother Abel, "Let us go out to the field."
And when they were in the field, Cain rose up against his
brother Abel, and killed him. Then the LORD said to Cain,
"Where is your brother Abel?" He said, "I do not know; am
I my brother's keeper?" And the LORD said, "What have you
done? Listen; your brother's blood is crying out to me from
the ground!"

Genesis 4:8-10

This is almost a frightening scripture to read, a more-than-sobering hymn to sing or contemplate singing. It is all so modern. The scripture reading, with minor variations of the characters (the Lord is not a common District Attorney or member of the police force), could be a lead story in almost any newspaper you pick up. Violence, accusations, and denials are the daily grist of the newspapers and the evening news shows. Of course God weeps, as do we all—unless we are inured against weeping because we have heard these stories so often.

So why a hymn about it? Because it happens, and because we are, all of us, our brother's and our sister's keeper. And these acts of jealousy and rivalry take place within our families and, yea verily, within our churches, which are supposed to be sanctuaries of love and forgiveness. It is not too much to say that God grieves as should we who are members of these communities.

Of course there are things to weep about. There will be disharmony in all communities. But can we face them, talk about them, get outside help if we need it? Can we be penitent and forgiving? Can we make a fresh start?

Then God's heart will lift. And so will ours.

Prayer: Thou who knowest our inmost thoughts, cleanse us from evil. Make us whole again. Amen.

Out of the Depths

#2136 in *The Faith We Sing*

Out of the depths I cry to you, O LORD. / Lord, hear my voice!

Psalm 130:1-2

The writer here is being more specific about "the depths" than is often the case with hymns or pleas for help in time of sorrow. Much more attention has been paid lately to the "delayed costs" of sorrows incurred in childhood or youth. One does not necessarily heal from old wounds by the passage of time. As the writer acknowledges, they often have a bearing on everything we do in the present.

In addition, the writer has supplied alternative words for the second line of the first stanza, to use in cases where they would be more appropriate than the general plea for help with past wounds.

She also acknowledges the need to speak of the unspeakable. How hard it is to crack open the shell of a painful memory, but sometimes that is the only way healing can begin.

It is also important to have people to whom we can trust the revelation of these hurts. It is here that the community of faith can be the place of disclosure; knowing that our trust will not be betrayed, our painful secrets can be disclosed in safety.

And, perhaps most profoundly, the light of God can both illumine and heal. Perhaps we shall be able to shed our burdens here, or gather the courage to seek professional help if that is necessary.

But the hope that is expressed is boundless: "Dance through our lives and loves; anoint with Spirit flame." To those who wondered whether, out of their depths, they would ever be able to dance again, the grace of God in the community of faith may be the healing beginning for those first halting steps.

Prayer: Thou who knowest our need more than we do, grant us your healing power. Amen.

Would I Have Answered When You Called

#2137 in *The Faith We Sing*

As he walked by the Sea of Galilee, he saw two brothers. . . .
And he said to them, "Follow me. . . ." Immediately they left
their nets and followed him.

Matthew 4:18-20

I suppose it is a question we have all asked ourselves: "How would I have responded to Jesus?" Not only if he had called me to be a disciple, but in the crowds that gathered around him, or in the smaller encounters with only a few, would I have turned away, a lot on my mind? Would I have turned away from this man in simple shepherd's clothing, sandals on his feet, trying to change the whole orientation of my comfortable, accustomed life?

I remember, years ago, when my children were adolescents, a poster in which a slightly unkempt-looking man (with sandals, even!) was pictured above the word "Wanted." I don't remember how the "Wanted" was elaborated, but the message was clear: The figure represented Jesus, and he was being accused of challenging the authorities, healing on the sabbath, and in general, causing disruption in society. It was a picture favored by thoughtful adolescents, realizing, perhaps for the first time, the radical nature of Jesus' message.

Response to Jesus is not a simple question. We know of charismatic figures (Jim Jones comes to mind) who have led their followers to evil and death. Perhaps the divining rod is in the message, and in the sense we get of who this stranger is, talking of God and love and justice, embodying these principles in his own life.

We don't know what our response to Jesus would be. We do know our lives would never be the same—just as they are affected now by having met him somewhere, and then again, and again.

Prayer: Holy God, may we listen when you call, may we follow where you lead. Amen.

Oh, I Know the Lord's Laid His Hands on Me

#2139 in *The Faith We Sing*

A leper . . . knelt before him, saying, "Lord, if you choose, you can make me clean." He stretched out his hand and touched him, saying, "I do choose. Be made clean!"
Matthew 8:2-3

Fortunately, with modern medicine, leprosy is no longer the curse it was in Jesus' time. But all kinds of illnesses cry out for healing—including addictions to alcohol, drugs, and overeating, and other illnesses that seem to have a psychological component (and we are finding a psychological component to more illnesses all the time). Yet leprosy was almost an assured death sentence. And in response to the man's cry, torn from his heart in faith, Jesus' touch made him well.

The jubilation and astonishment reflected in this hymn led the man to equate Jesus' power to heal with a power to wash away all his sins. He spoke better than he knew. Certainly not all illnesses are a result of sinful living, but some are. And the connection in the man's mind was very clear—though modern medicine might challenge this particular assumption—that leprosy is associated with sinful living. It would have made no difference: The man was desperately ill and came to Jesus in faith, and his faith was rewarded.

The third stanza carries a cautionary note against the assumption that you can live a sinful life and then somehow "pray it away." And then the fourth stanza returns us to the miracle of Jesus' healing.

There is another element here that begs for our attention. Matthew writes, "He stretched out his hand and touched him." The ministry of healing touch seems to expand the power of one to heal another—not only with Jesus, but with you and me as well.

Prayer: We are grateful, O God, for your power to heal. May we be healers, too. Amen.

41

I've Got Peace Like a River

#2145 in *The Faith We Sing*

"Peace I leave with you; my peace I give to you. I do not give to you as the world gives. Do not let your hearts be troubled, and do not let them be afraid."

John 14:27

This African American spiritual is a wonderfully soothing hymn to sing, especially if you have a river you've been happily familiar with since childhood. The memory and security of those earlier days will probably enrich this song for you, even before you start to sing! In these words, you can "see" it all—the riverbanks, rocky or lush with green bushes, perhaps a ride on a riverboat, or even a swim. "Peace like a river" is going back home.

And then comes "joy like a fountain." What an image of beauty and gracefulness. Maybe you even had permission to sit on the edge and dabble your toes in the water. Or, on a more mundane level, recall the ring of the hose set on the side lawn, and the delicious pleasure of running through that fountain.

And the last stanza extends to "love like an ocean." Those of us who have lived close enough to the ocean have watched its many moods, marveled at the distances we can scarcely fathom—a boundless body of water, constant and unending. And can we imagine a love like that, that we can carry in our souls. Love overflowing. Love never ending. Love like an ocean.

Love playful as a fountain.

Love that winds through the passage of the riverbank, coming from upriver, flowing onward for as far as the eye can see.

To carry these images in one's heart is to know joy and peace. No wonder we love to sing this hymn.

Prayer: God of the river, the fountain, the ocean, we thank you for these gifts. Amen.

His Eye Is on the Sparrow

#2146 in *The Faith We Sing*

"Are not five sparrows sold for two pennies? Yet not one of them is forgotten in God's sight. But even the hairs of your head are all counted. Do not be afraid."

Luke 12:6-7

Many of us, when we sing this song, hear in our mind the lyrical voice of Ethel Waters, for whom this was a favorite song. Knowing little myself of the life of Ethel Waters, nonetheless I feel her as a kind of companion of the way, and her voice, singing somewhere in the back of my head, offers a resonance and companionship that enriches the song for me.

When I think of God speaking through birds, I see a pair of cardinals pecking at birdseed outside the glass wall of the patio next to the room where I work. It was during the months after our daughter died, when I, in my desolation, was hungry for any sign at all that God cared for us.

One morning, as I began my work, the words of a song kept going through my head. "Feed the birds . . . feed the birds. . . . " The song persisted until finally, almost in impatience to get past it, I got some birdseed, scattered it on the snow-covered patio, and returned to my desk.

Partway through the morning, still engulfed in my sadness, I turned and saw, just outside the glass wall, a red cardinal and his mate, hopping about and pecking at the seed—the two of them, hopping, pecking. Suddenly my heart was light: it was as though they had been sent to me. They stayed for a long time, hopping to a nearby limb, dropping back down, even looking through the glass where I watched, my eyes stinging with gratitude for their presence, their life.

They came often that winter—I was sure it was the same two—appearing to come when I needed them most.

Prayer: God, who comes to us through the sparrow—or the cardinal—we rejoice in any assurance of your presence and your love. Amen.

Over My Head

#2148 in *The Faith We Sing*

For your steadfast love is as high as the heavens; / your faithfulness extends to the clouds. / Be exalted, O God, above the heavens. / Let your glory be over all the earth.
Psalm 57:10-11

This is truly a "feel good" hymn. We are all surrounded by mystery, and we wonder: What does it mean? In this hymn, the writer is exulting in his sense that what he is hearing in the mystery, the "music in the air," is none other than the God of all the universe. For how could such celestial sounds come from Nowhere, from Nothing?

This music comes even in silence—the music of God ringing in the inner ear, even when the world seems still. Music in silence? It is the voice of God, singing to the believer's ear, assuring one who listens that "there must be a God somewhere."

And in times of personal anguish, when one is feeling alone and lonely—even then there's music in the air. Company, solace, an unseen presence of love—"There must be a God somewhere."

And last in this hymn, to the attuned ear, just the thought of Jesus puts music in the air, transforms the uncertainty and silence and loneliness into the music of faith. In very truth, "there must be a God somewhere."

Part of the beauty of this hymn is its breadth of understanding. For all of us, at different times in our lives, the world seems silent and unresponsive. We don't need to give reasons. We all have times of loneliness. We don't have to explain why or make excuses. And to "think on Jesus" can be anything from an inner replay of Jesus' life and death, to a flash of love. The "music in the air" is pervasive; it fills the universe. "There must be a God somewhere."

Prayer: God, help us to keep listening, so that in all circumstances, we hear the music. Amen.

Just a Closer Walk with Thee

#2158 in *The Faith We Sing*

Even though I walk through the darkest valley, / I fear no evil; / for you are with me.

Psalm 23:4

This is a hymn of crying out for reassurance, for the companionship of Jesus when things are looking sad or when we are in need of the ultimate support that Jesus can bring to us. Maybe we ourselves don't even know why life—and our own inner poise—seems particularly fragile at such times. Or maybe we do know. I have sung this hymn under both sets of circumstances and have felt my spirit lifted and strengthened and made calmer in the singing.

The words could scarcely be simpler, which is probably just what we need when we feel burdened or worried, often by causes unknown to us. The exact cause or causes are not important. What is important is that the hymn says in words what we have been sensing but find hard to articulate: I need you. Be with me. In the confusions of my life, stand beside me. Your presence will heal my brokenness, my uncertainty, my pain.

And the ultimate plea, voiced in confidence: "When I am crossing from life unto death, be my guide, be with me, help me over."

The tempo, the rhythm, of this hymn also has much to do with its power. The mood is contemplative—a recognition of need, and a plea for help where ultimate help can be found. In such a mood, a fast pace would be incongruent with the message. The words are simple, expressive of our own deep longings. Slowly, prayerfully, we sing, confident that the One to whom the words are addressed listens from a heart of unfathomable love and presence.

Prayer: "Just a closer walk with thee, grant it, Jesus, is my plea." Amen.

Grace Alone

#2162 in *The Faith We Sing*

For by grace you have been saved through faith, and this is not your own doing; it is the gift of God.

Ephesians 2:8

When I read through the words of this hymn, two things come to mind. One is the sentence from Georges Bernanos novel *The Diary of a Country Priest*, in which the protagonist says, at the end of the book, "All is grace."

The second thing that comes to mind is a scene that took place several years ago. My husband and I were in church, and one point in the service a woman rose to sing. She had been a singer all of her adult life. She had struggled with many circumstances: poverty, discrimination, turbulent family relationships. She was struggling now with cancer, and she knew—and we knew—that she would die. We were astonished that she could summon the strength and courage to sing.

The song was, "Lord, Don't Move This Mountain"—her rich contralto voice clear and strong, asking the Lord in song for nothing more than the strength to climb. Except for her voice, the room was utterly still. She sang the song through to the end. Her hand caught at the side of the lectern. She sat down. It was her last time to come to church. She was transfigured, and so were we.

We all have our stories, times when we have felt the indwelling presence of God so strongly that it seemed almost to pass through our skin and make us one with creation. Or times when we have seen in the life of others a radiance and peace that seem totally inconsistent with the difficult circumstances of their life. This is the "grace alone" that this hymn celebrates.

Prayer: Eternal God, may we recognize your hand in the blessings that are ours. Amen.

Here Am I

#2178 in *The Faith We Sing*

"Then they also will answer, 'Lord, when was it that we saw you hungry or thirsty or a stranger or naked or sick or in prison, and did not take care of you?' Then he will answer them, 'Truly I tell you, just as you did not do it to one of the least of these, you did not do it to me.'"

Matthew 25:44-45

In this hymn, Jesus confronts us with the unavoidable question, "Where are you when I—in the person of the homeless, the hungry, the jobless, the mistreated—am standing in line, needing help?"

The scenes the writer describes are all too familiar, particularly if we live in large cities where people are forced to sleep under bridges, live in substandard housing, and have inadequate heating; and there don't seem to be enough jobs to go around. The "pensioners and strikers" are not included in Matthew's list of the destitute, but they are often equally deprived.

Many of our cities and churches are now providing food programs, hospitality on cold winter nights, and better housing efforts. But much more needs to be done.

The third stanza offers hope for alleviating some of these conditions. "Where two or three are gathered, ready to be altered, sharing wine and bread"—Jesus is surely there. Where there are those who are moved by the preaching that they hear to lead a different kind of life and to share more of their goods and services with those who need them, and, in so doing, find that their lives take on new meaning—Jesus is surely there, too. Here, inescapably, as with the first two stanzas, the question is put baldly, with no alleviating, moderating escape clauses: "Where are you?"

Prayer: God, help us face the difficult questions, for in sharing there is abundant life. Amen.

Live in Charity *(Ubi Caritas)*

#2179 in *The Faith We Sing*

Love is patient; love is kind; love is not envious or boast-ful or arrogant or rude. . . . It bears all things, believes all things, hopes all things, endures all things. Love never ends. . . . And now faith, hope, and love abide, these three; and the greatest of these is love.

1 Corinthians 13:4-13

This hymn exudes a kind of peace present in few other hymns I know. It has surely passed the test of time, as it is taken from a prayer Christians have prayed for more than a thousand years.

It has a unique place in our modern history, coming as it does from the Taizé community, the ecumenical monas-tic movement that began in occupied France during World War II.

It is here presented in English, accompanied by the orig-inal Latin translation, though probably more often than not it is sung in the Latin, simple enough for anyone to "catch on" to.

Furthermore, the melody is so simple. The third phrase of the melody is almost identical to the first, and a sooth-ing quality pervades the whole piece of music. The words, too, with their radical promise, "God will dwell with you," seem to offer, in their very simplicity, an attainable goal. They are, indeed, the essence of the gospel.

One feels that singing this over and over several times (which is often done) cannot help making one a better Christian—certainly a more tranquil one—though some of the tranquility may dissipate as one takes specific steps to "live in charity." But if living in charity is an outgrowth of this hymn, it will be charity deeply rooted in peace.

Prayer: We thank you God, for those who have kept this hymn alive for us. May its message pervade our lives. Amen.

Why Stand So Far Away, My God?

#2180 in *The Faith We Sing*

Why, O LORD, do you stand far off? / Why do you hide yourself in times of trouble?

Psalm 10:1

This is a complaint that goes as far back as humankind has voiced any words to God. We hear it in many of the psalms. We hear it at length in the book of Job, where his interlocutors are trying to discover the source of his misery. We hear it on the streets and back alleys of our cities, in the overcrowded homeless shelters, in the courtrooms where justice seems captive to the wealthy and powerful. We hear it, in ultimate terms, in Jesus' plea from the cross, "My God, my God, why have you forsaken me?"

And probably, in times of extreme distress, we ourselves have felt that God is standing "far away."

There is a special accusation here, too: *You did it for them; why don't you do it for me?* Or, since this seems more a corporate than an individual cry and accusation, *You did it "in ages past" for them—defending the powerless against oppressors. Now, in these times, why do you not come to the aid of the oppressed?* (I'm not so sure the oppressed in ages past, like Job, didn't have their own unanswered complaints against God.)

There will probably always be cries for help for those in need. But if there is any clue to at least a partial answer to such cries, perhaps it is found at the end of the last stanza: "Come, help *us* (italics mine) stop the flow of blood!" So perhaps it is we who are at least partly responsible for all of these miscarriages of justice. Perhaps it is we who must help bring about changes in society to "let terror reign no more."

Prayer: Eternal God, who wills justice for all, help us to be agents of deliverance. Amen.

49

For One Great Peace

#2185 in *The Faith We Sing*

Now there are varieties of gifts, but the same Spirit. . . .
To each is given the manifestation of the Spirit for the
common good.

1 Corinthians 12:4, 7

Often in our churches (and in our consciences) the "real" work of the church, the "real" vocation for a Christian is not what we consider to be our own calling, our true vocation. Wise and good friends will try to reassure us, "Writing is a Christian vocation"—or sculpture, or carpentry (we have a good model for that one), or dancing or gardening or homemaking. We listen gratefully, and we know they are right, but often the anxiety returns: *Shouldn't I be out feeding the hungry, gathering petitions, tending to the needs of the poor?*

But perhaps ours are different gifts. Someone has said, "Why is it that because we enjoy doing something, it isn't Christian work?" We see the folly in that, but it is easy to think that the really committed Christians spend their time primarily visiting prisons or working with those who are poor and in need.

This hymn reminds us that there are many ways to serve God, and some of them don't involve wearing a preacher's robe, or carrying a placard, or collecting voter registrations or signatures on a petition. Instead, it can be someone wearing the casual clothing of a young mother; an architect tending to the intricate design details of a building; a writer struggling at a desk.

The story is told that, in the famous picture by Durer of two hands raised in prayer, the model was a friend of Durer's who spent his life at manual labor so that Durer could pursue his art. A Christian society needs its artists as it needs its social workers, its preachers—and its choir members.

Prayer: Eternal Creator, who has given each of us skills to pursue and talents to use, be with us on our journeys. Amen.

Song of Hope
(Canto de Esperanza)

#2186 in *The Faith We Sing*

May the God of hope fill you with all joy and peace in believing, so that you may abound in hope by the power of the Holy Spirit.

Romans 15:13

This hymn, originally from Argentina, tells us that two things are necessary if we are to be faithful workers for Christ: We need to have hope that does not flag, and we need to work for justice and peace.

Just as we cannot keep up our enthusiasm on a project of our own undertaking without hope, so we cannot continue to seek justice and peace in our communities, our nations, our world, without hope.

One way we build up our hope, keep it going, is by singing. Another is by praying. Daily prayer keeps us energized for our tasks. So this "Song of Hope" is part song, part prayer.

I recall, back in the 1960s and 1970s, attending some meetings of an interracial, intercollegiate network of students dedicated to trying, by nonviolent means, to bring about a greater degree of peace and justice in our troubled society. Members of this group were often physically and verbally abused. Often their lives were in danger.

I wondered where they got their staying power—until, at one of their meetings, they stood and began to sing. "We shall overcome," they sang—their song of hope—and I knew where at least part of their power came from.

So do we, in our work for peace and justice, need songs of hope and prayers for sustenance and power in doing God's work.

Prayer: God of Power, God of Hope and Love, may we keep the faith, singing as we go. Amen.

Now It Is Evening

#2187 in *The Faith We Sing*

"As the Father has loved me, so I have loved you; abide in my love. If you keep my commandments, you will abide in my love, just as I have kept my Father's commandments and abide in his love. . . . This is my commandment, that you love one another as I have loved you."

John 15:9-12

Each of the four stanzas of this hymn begins with images of peace and contentment.

The first calls up the lights of the city—lights being turned on in homes, lights turned on for the evening meal or a nighttime story hour, street lights turned on to make the cities and sidewalks safe. They remind us: Christ is our light.

But wait! There are people for whom the coming of evening means loneliness. The true light of Christ means that we reach out to them, become their neighbor.

Likewise there is a duality with the three remaining stanzas. The image of sleeping children may remind us that Christ is our peace. But is there something more? There are people neglected, uncared for. To reach out to them in some way will bring Christ's peace.

The cozy evening scene with food on the table often means the fellowship of the family gathered around, the exchanging of stories of the day. But again, there are those who are hungry, who haven't the food we so take for granted. Who will feed them? "Where there is sharing Christ is our life."

And in the cozy evening, we remember that Christ is our friend. But there are strangers, people without friends. Who will befriend them? Who will welcome them into the circle of warmth? "Where there's a welcome Christ is our friend."

Prayer: God of the fortunate and unfortunate, help us share with those in need. Amen.

A Mother Lined a Basket

#2189 in *The Faith We Sing*

The woman conceived and bore a son. . . . When she could hide him no longer she got a papyrus basket for him, and plastered it with bitumen and pitch; she put the child in it and placed it among the reeds on the bank of the river.
Exodus 2:2-3

If you look down at the bottom of the page on which this hymn is printed, you will see that three of the four Bible references given tell the story from one of the first three stanzas of the hymn.

The first baby laid in a lined basket is, of course, the infant Moses, a story that so captivated me as a child that I planned that when I grew up, if I had a baby boy, I would name him Moses. (I did grow up to have three baby boys, none of whom is named Moses—which just shows you can change your mind.)

The second is the child Samuel. His mother Hannah, who had been childless for many years, brought him to the temple as soon as he was weaned, to be consecrated to the Lord. How she must have yearned for him, but she gave him to Eli for nurture and training, because "she had such faith to give." Many of us remember the story of Samuel's being called repeatedly in the night, how when he went to Eli, thinking Eli had called him, Eli said, "No, I didn't call you. Go back to bed." This kept happening until Eli realized it was the Lord's call. So Samuel became a prophet.

The third child, laid in a manger lined with straw, is of course the infant Jesus, destined to grow up to be the Savior of the world; again, a child of one's heart given over to fulfill a great destiny. Three mothers. This has been said by many, but we who are parents know the truth of the hymn's line, "The hardest part of loving is learning to let go."

Prayer: Eternal God of Love, we thank you for these mothers and their sacrificial love. Amen.

Eternal Father, Strong to Save

#2191 in *The Faith We Sing*

They took him with them in the boat.... A great wind-storm arose ... so that the boat was already being swamped. But he was in the stern, asleep on the cushion.... He woke up and rebuked the wind.... Then the wind ceased.

Mark 4:36-39

This is a familiar story to us—how, in the howling storm, Jesus bid the wind and wave be still, and everyone was safe. This hymn is commonly known as the "Navy Hymn," which it is. However, it is not a hymn of aggression, a prayer for victory at sea, but a prayer for safety at sea, referring to the stories of Jesus calming the waters when the others on board thought surely they would drown.

During World War II, I was a student at Mount Holyoke College, and often, at the close of vespers on Sunday evening, one part of the congregation would sing this hymn and, at the same time, juxtaposed against these words, the other part of the congregation would sing what was known as the "Mount Holyoke Hymn," which begins, "There's a light upon the mountain and the day is at the spring." We would come to the end of our two hymns at exactly the same time. It was a stirring occasion for us all, perhaps made more so by the fact that a contingent of WAVES, the Navy's women's auxiliary, was stationed at Mount Holyoke, and we saw them come and go each day, in their navy skirts and gold-trimmed jackets.

I'm sure no one, hearing about this, would think it a very likely combination of hymns—one a plea for safety at sea, the other anticipating the triumph of God's righteousness. In the words of the current idiom, "You had to be there." But having been there, I still feel a stirring when a congregation begins, "Eternal Father, strong to save," and in the back of my mind, I hear in splendid counterpart,

"There's a light upon the mountain." Holy moments, at sea and on land.

Prayer: God of the land and the rolling sea, we pray for safety in life's storms. Amen.

O Freedom

#2194 in *The Faith We Sing*

For freedom Christ has set us free. Stand firm, therefore, and do not submit again to a yoke of slavery.

Galatians 5:1

This African American spiritual was a much-used rallying cry during the early Civil Rights movement, and its echo stays with us to this day where there are still injustices and cries for freedom, in this country, as well as in many countries around the world.

The hymn is also a way in present-day churches where people of many national origins, including African, gather in worship, to express in rousing song our solidarity with one another—now, and in a past we cannot relive but can certainly try to imagine. I, for one, feel privileged to join in this song with the African American sisters and brothers in our congregation.

The song has a broader meaning, too, of course. We can rejoice together over freedom from any bondage—addictions conquered, abusive relationships repudiated, fears calmed, faith reclaimed. And if we are faltering on the edges of any of these or other bondages, this exhilarating embracing of freedom, this prospect of going home in freedom to God, should strengthen our resolve.

The declarations of freedom—"no more moaning . . . no more weeping"—at first focus on repudiating enslavement and are stated in the negative. But then the proclamations break forth with more positive signs of freedom achieved: "There'll be singing . . . shouting . . . praying over me." Now the words, as well as the music, move us from a sometimes reticent, quiet repentance, to a real exultation of body and spirit that reverberates with the joy of victory won, and again paves the way to "go home to my Lord and be free."

Prayer: God, stand by our side, hold our hand, urge us forward in our fight for freedom. Amen.

Lord of All Hopefulness

#2197 in *The Faith We Sing*

For in hope we were saved. Now hope that is seen is not hope. For who hopes for what is seen? But if we hope for what we do not see, we wait for it with patience.

Romans 8:24-25

This hymn follows with beautiful similitude the varying moods of the day. My brother, recently retired, tells me that one of the aspects of retirement that pleases him most is "being able, on waking, to invent the day." That doesn't always happen—commitments have been made, plans need to be carried out. But his words gave me a new sense of the adventure retirement can bring—space for the unknown, hope that the day will turn out to be a good day.

A friend, also of retirement age, passed on a piece of advice: "If you're going to start something new, start before ten o'clock." I knew just what she meant. If the day is already edging toward noon—well, it's a little late to start something new—a new story, a new project, a new attack on the closet that needs to be totally reorganized.

Our days assume their own rhythm, and, as hopefulness (that the unknown will turn out to be "a good thing") accompanies our waking, so we hope that energy and resolve carry us through the hours of daily work.

And then as the workday winds down, we hope to be blessed as we return home or as we welcome the home-comers if our work has been "home." And we hope too that preparing and eating the evening meal, and getting the children ready for bed, can be done with an extra infusion of the love we bear for one another.

And then comes the blessedness of contentment and healing sleep.

Prayer: May the assurance of God's love go with us through the stages of each day. Amen.

57

Without Seeing You

#2206 in *The Faith We Sing*

Jesus said to him, "Have you believed because you have seen me? Blessed are those who have not seen and yet have come to believe."

John 20:29

In this hymn, the singers' assertions of faith—confidence that their dwelling place with Christ is secure just as the sparrow will surely find its nest, confidence that in unseen pastures, by unseen waters, believers will find their rest—testify to the power and strength of God.

They have not seen him, yet they love him. They have not touched him, yet they are eager for his embrace. They do not know him, yet they follow. They cannot see him, yet they believe.

We think with astonishment of the power Jesus must have carried in his person when we read of his saying to those fishermen, "Come with me, and I will make you fishers of men." And they dropped their nets, just like that, and followed him. They gave over their lives to him, their futures to him—on no more evidence than the simple fact of his presence, the words he spoke.

Once, many years ago, I heard a sermon by Clarence Jordan, who founded Koinonia Farm, an interracial, Christian farming community in Georgia in the early days of the Civil Rights movement. And I understood, in at least a partial way, how a person could present himself in such a winning and attractive way that one might, indeed, leave all, and go with him.

There have been, in recent history, horrible examples of charismatic leaders who exerted such power, attracting followers and then leading them to their death. So discernment is necessary here. But there was something about Jesus that even those who had never seen him became his followers. Such blessings he himself must have emanated that, not knowing him, they would embrace him with their lives!

Prayer: Gracious and loving God, we who have not seen come to you with open arms. Amen.

How Long, O Lord

#2209 in *The Faith We Sing*

How Long, O LORD? Will you forget me forever? / How long will you hide your face from me? / How long must I bear pain in my soul, / and have sorrow in my heart all day long? . . . But I trusted in your steadfast love; / my heart shall rejoice in your salvation. / I will sing to the LORD, / because he has dealt bountifully with me.

Psalm 13:1-6

This hymn moves through a sequence of moods with which many of us are familiar. If you have sustained a grievous and unexpected loss in your family, or in your vocation, or in anything else that matters profoundly to you, you will understand the despair and the sense of God's absence that sometimes comes when you search and search for some sign of God's redeeming love, some assurance of God's healing presence. And apparently you look to no avail. Has God forgotten that you exist? Night and day you scan the horizon of your mind, and you do not find any relief.

And then one day—it may come suddenly or slip quietly into your heart—you realize that life feels different than it did a month or two ago. Perhaps the song of a bird will seem beautiful again. Perhaps a friend you've not expected knocks at your door and says, "I was going by and I thought I'd stop and see how you're doing." And you throw your arms around this friend and sob out your grief, and suddenly you feel lighter. Or perhaps some hymn at church, or a part of a sermon that seems to speak especially to you, will restore your spirit and you will be able to believe again. You find yourself believing the words the members of a lay mission team were encouraged to say to those who seemed ready to hear it, "God

loves you, and I love you." *Yes! It could be true! I am not forgotten. God has not turned away from me!*
And you realize that you have begun to trust again.

Prayer: O God, who has known sorrow at the waywardness of your children, stand with me in my sorrow, and help me learn to love again. Amen.

My Life Flows On

#2212 in *The Faith We Sing*

Let the word of Christ dwell in you richly; teach and admonish one another in all wisdom; and with gratitude in your hearts sing psalms, hymns, and spiritual songs to God.
Colossians 3:16

"How can I keep from singing?"

Have you ever felt like that—that you had such joy in your heart that you couldn't keep from singing? When?

When you and your love decided to marry?

When you wanted a baby so badly and the pregnancy test turned out positive?

When you finally got the job of your dreams?

When the biopsy told you there was nothing to worry about?

When the book you've worked on for years finally found its way to the right publisher?

We have had such moments, and we rejoice in them deeply. But it is a different sort of cause that gives this hymn writer a lift so great that, whatever happens, he cannot lose the profound confidence and joy in life that bursts forth in "How can I keep from singing?" This is the supreme confidence that the music, the echoes, the songs in the night reflect the new creation in Christ Jesus, and that no storm, no loss of comfort, no gathering dark can displace the peace of Christ, "a fountain ever springing."

And when we join in this hymn of praise and thanksgiving, our mood, however low it may have been when we began, lifts with the writer's, and we sing: "The peace of Christ makes fresh my heart, a fountain ever springing! All things are mine since I am his! How can I keep from singing?"

Prayer: God who has put a new song in our hearts, we sing in astonishment and gratitude. Amen.

They'll Know We Are Christians by Our Love

#2223 in *The Faith We Sing*

"I give you a new commandment, that you love one another. Just as I have loved you, you also should love one another. By this everyone will know that you are my disciples, if you have love for one another."

John 13:34-35

Will they know we are Christians, when they read that a church is trying to break away from a denomination because of differences in belief and practice, or that a group within the church is denied the sacraments because they come from a different tradition? These publicly aired disagreements are irritating to nonbelievers, and painful to believers.

But they are fractions of the whole story. They do not tell of the newly confirmed parishioner who stands with tears of gratitude in her eyes as she says, half in laughter, half in tears, "I've been looking for this church for twenty years. I don't know why it's taken me so long to find you." And the congregation gathers around to embrace her, to welcome her "home."

What is hard in matters of controversy is that, in most instances, people on both sides of a question believe they are acting out of love, doing as Jesus would have them do. Perhaps this is where love also makes itself manifest, that we love one another *in* our differences, and if the love is not returned—well, that's a story at least as old as Christ's struggles with the Pharisees and with the Roman soldiers who put him to death, even as he prayed to God, "Father, forgive them; for they do not know what they are doing."

But, on the bright side, come to a church community (and there are many of them) where shelter and food are offered to the homeless on cold winter nights, where a schedule is made out so there will always be someone to sit with a person dying of cancer, where the sacred meal of Communion binds people to one another and to God; and after embraces are exchanged and tears are dried and laughter is shared, even a casual passerby would "know we are Christians by our love."

Prayer: God, who has made of one blood all nations of the earth, unite us in your love. Amen.

Lead On, O Cloud of Presence

#2234 in *The Faith We Sing*

The LORD went in front of them in a pillar of cloud by day, to lead them along the way, and in a pillar of fire by night, to give them light, so that they might travel by day and by night. Neither the pillar of cloud by day nor the pillar of fire by night left its place in front of the people.

Exodus 13:21-22

This tune may be familiar to singers and readers as the hymn "Lead On, O King Eternal," but this is a far less militaristic hymn. This is a procession, led by the same miraculously leading pillar of cloud by day and pillar of fire by night, but there is no mention of battle here.

The fear of the unknown is here as the Israelites, freed from slavery, venture into the desert wilderness. Did they wonder whether they were doing the right thing, following this strange apparition? Might it lead them to destruction? Yet they followed in trust—for what else could this be but God leading them on the path they were destined to follow? They acknowledge the uncertainty of the voyage—yet they never lose sight of the promise that they are God's people. And then that wonderful line, a thought echoed by Christians (and others, as well), that their home is the journey itself.

They recognize, as Moses did when he viewed the promised land, that they themselves may never reach their foreordained destination. But their prayer is that their sons and daughters will, still led on by the cloud in the daytime, the pillar of fire in the night—that their descendants may achieve what has been the hope of the people all along, to reach a land of justice with mercy, and ruled by a law of love.

Prayer: Eternal God, guide us still to achieve a land where justice, tempered by love, prevails. Amen.

Walk with Me

#2242 in *The Faith We Sing*

But Moses said to God, "Who am I that I should go to Pharaoh, and bring the Israelites out of Egypt?" He said, "I will be with you; and this shall be the sign for you that it is I who sent you: when you have brought the people out of Egypt, you shall worship God on this mountain."

Exodus 3:11-12

How many times have we been asked to do things we don't really want to do, but feel we "ought"? Someone has suggested that we reach a state of mature integrity when we can say to ourselves, "No more 'shoulds.'"

But that's only part of the story, because we know there are tasks that are truly ours. There is a distinction, and we probably don't always make the right choice. But as the stories in this hymn tell us—stories of Moses, of Peter, of Mary—the closer we feel to God, the more likely we are to know what is right for us. So it was for Moses, who tried to dissuade God: "I am not a leader. I am not an eloquent man." So it was for Peter, who tried to divert Jesus from his holy calling and ended up a leader in Christ's church. So it was with Mary, who wondered how she, who wasn't even married, could be given the great honor of bearing God's Son.

And so it is with you and me, if we discern that a role we would rather avoid is really God's will.

And how did these historic figures—and how do we—summon the courage and strength to carry out a God-given mission? By staying close to God. "Walk with me," God urges, "I will walk with you." And we do, and God does, and as God's people we are able in faith to support one another, and our hearts overflow with gratitude for the blessing we really weren't sure we wanted at all!

Prayer: God, teach me what is truly my work, and then let me feel you walking close beside me. Amen.

Come! Come! Everybody Worship (Vengan Todos Adoremos)

#2271 in *The Faith We Sing*

Remember the sabbath day, and keep it holy. Six days you shall labor and do all your work. But the seventh day is a sabbath to the LORD your God. . . . For in six days the LORD made heaven and earth, the sea and all that is in them, but rested the seventh day; therefore the LORD blessed the sabbath day and consecrated it.

Exodus 20:8-11

This hymn, the refrain printed in Spanish as well as in English, was originally intended as a song for children, and it has the lift and buoyancy—and fast pace—that children enjoy. (I have heard my nine-year-old granddaughter sing this with her choir, and, as the saying goes, "Their hearts were in it!") Also, the words are not complicated but have enough variety in the stanzas to hold children's attention and to keep the song interesting.

The language too is suited for children, as in the first stanza: "Worship and remember to keep the Sabbath day. Take a rest and think of God; put your work away."

In this time of our common life, many people are coming to realize that the frenetic pace we have been keeping—often for seven days of the week—has left us no feel for sabbath rest, let alone for preserving the prescribed hours for sabbath.

Some may remember the film *Chariots of Fire,* in which the hero gave up his chance to win an important race because it was to be run on Sunday. During the last several years, a number of books and articles have appeared pointing out that we do ourselves a disservice—physical as well as mental and spiritual—by treating the sabbath as just another day to jam as much into as we can, rather than using it as a God-prescribed opportunity for re-creating ourselves.

Prayer: God, help us make time for sabbath rest, for our own and for our world's sake. Amen.

May You Run and Not Be Weary

2281 in *The Faith We Sing*

*But those who wait for the L*ORD *shall renew their strength, / they shall mount up with wings like eagles, / they shall run and not be weary, / they shall walk and not faint.*

Isaiah 40:31

This is a familiar scripture, though it appears a bit differently in the hymn. But familiar as it is, it casts its own glow, has its own meaning in this song.

As a writer, my first use of these familiar phrases came as I was concluding an article about a weekend work camp I attended years ago as a recent college graduate. I had a Monday through Friday job in a publishing office, but this was a weekend commitment—Friday night through Sunday morning—and I went partly because a friend had invited me to come along.

It was a Quaker-sponsored project, and we slept on cots in the basement of a church. Our work project was helping people in substandard apartments paint and otherwise "fix up" their dwelling places. On Friday, after some supper and some silence, we were given a "painting lesson," as well as some background on these people's lives and the importance of treating them as equal workers with us. On Saturday, we took sack lunches with us, and at the end of the day we came back to the church to have supper and to tell our stories of the day.

I had painted with an apartment resident, and we talked of things women talk about. But what surprised me, as the group gathered for supper, was that I was not tired. It was then that I heard these words in a new way: "Those who wait for the Lord shall renew their strength," and "May you run [or paint] and not be weary. May your life be filled with joy."

Prayer: God, may our hearts be filled with song, and hope, and strength. And may the roads we travel always lead us home. Amen.

Index